THEN & NOW

WELLFLEET

Opposite: In this vintage postcard from about 1930, the Higgins oyster shed in Wellfleet Harbor is seen. The Lemon Pie Cottages are on the upper right, overlooking what is now the town marina.

THEN & NOW

WELLFLEET

Daniel Lombardo

ALONG THE SHORE ROAD, WELLFLEET, CAPE COD, MASS

Copyright © 2007 by Daniel Lombardo
ISBN 978-0-7385-4992-7

Library of Congress control number: 2006939751

Published by Arcadia Publishing
Charleston SC, Chicago IL, Portsmouth NH, San Francisco CA

Printed in the United States of America

For all general information contact Arcadia Publishing at:
Telephone 843-853-2070
Fax 843-853-0044
E-mail sales@arcadiapublishing.com
For customer service and orders:
Toll-Free 1-888-313-2665

Visit us on the Internet at www.arcadiapublishing.com

On the front cover: Duck Creek used to be the inner harbor of Wellfleet, busy with boats and oyster sheds. Today a sleepy old boat weathers on the shore. (Vintage photograph courtesy of the Wellfleet Historical Society, contemporary photograph by Daniel Lombardo.)

On the back cover: The Cape has suffered some 3,000 shipwrecks; this Lower Cape wreck is from around 1900. (Courtesy of the Wellfleet Historical Society.)

CONTENTS

ACKNOWLEDGMENTS

Deep thanks to Karen Banta, the Wellfleet Historical Society, Joan Coughlin, Michael Parlante, David Rego, Sue and Bob Gross, Elaine McIlroy, Denny O'Connell, and the Reverend Kenneth C. Roscoe. Unless otherwise noted, all vintage photographs are courtesy of the Wellfleet Historical Society, and all contemporary photographs are by Daniel Lombardo.

INTRODUCTION

At the southern edge of Wellfleet Harbor there used to be an island called Billingsgate. The families, houses, cattle, schoolhouse, and lighthouse are all gone now. The islanders used to tell of a mysterious light that appeared over the water between the Billingsgate and the Brewster shores. They said the light came from "Lumpkin's Hole," a famous spot for hunting pilot whales, an area with a white sandy bottom, surrounded by eel grass. When a fisherman named Lumpkin disappeared, his body was found in the hole. Since then, they said, the light from his lantern was seen above the spot

Until my wife, Karen, and I bought our Wellfleet cottage on Chequessett Neck Road, I thought mysterious tales, eccentric characters, and the wild Cape Cod landscape of old Wellfleet were gone. But strange doings persist. Today I open the *Cape Codder* newspaper and read that the owner of Finely J. P.'s Restaurant went to the Wellfleet Selectboard and requested a temporary closing of his own restaurant. The reason? An unexplained "echo problem."

Wellfleet has somehow remained, at heart, the small fishing village it always was. Granted, the town is overrun with vacationers for two months of the year, but most of the time it is left to the locals at Uncle Frank's, to the lobster boats, and to the shellfish fishermen. It is an isolated place at the outer end of a long-armed peninsula that bends and stretches into the Atlantic Ocean. When the tourists leave, the seabirds and seals of the Arctic return. Seals lie in the sun at Jeremy Point, and resident Wellfleeters go about living lives of their own invention.

As we grew accustomed to the pace and the ways of Wellfleet, it no longer seemed odd that a man lived on the harbor in a shack built on a raft, with pirate flags at one end and a hibachi at the other. We were, however, taken aback after we bought our place and read that Wellfleet had the highest murder rate in Massachusetts. Yes, there had been *one* murder in Wellfleet the year before. With a population of only about 2,500, that gave the town the highest per capita murder rate in the state. Muddying that distinction was the news that the murder had taken place elsewhere, and the body had been dumped in our town. It could not really be claimed as a true Wellfleet murder after all.

Wellfleeters have a wry sense of humor about life's absurdities, which seem to float in with the regularity of the tide. In 2004, something went wrong at noon on Independence Day. As the fireworks were being set up on Indian Point, people in the village across the water heard a deep rumbling and looked up to see a full fireworks show in broad daylight. Something set off the explosives, destroying a truck and starting a brush fire. The story made national news, and Wellfleet, relieved and a bit amused, put a photograph of the midday fireworks on the cover of that year's annual report.

Glance through the Cape Cod newspapers and you will get an idea of the rough-and-tumble of Wellfleet politics. Wellfleet's lively form of democracy is proudly exercised, but it is not for the thin-skinned. A recent news item noted Wellfleet's sense of "otherness": "If you think that Cape Cod is divided into three sections, upper, middle and lower, you're wrong. So says Selectman Gallagher. There's also 'outer Cape,' he said, 'and that's us.'" When Wellfleet attempted to hire a town administrator from off-Cape in 1997, the subsequent newspaper headline summed up the town's "this is us, take it or leave it" philosophy: "New Wellfleet Administrator Spends One Night, Flees—Kulow Came, She Saw, She Quit."

Unlike so many Cape Cod towns, Wellfleet has retained its small village atmosphere *and* the wild natural world of the outer beaches, the bay, and its ponds, marshes, and moors. More than 60 percent of Wellfleet is protected from development within the Cape Cod National Seashore. The Wellfleet Bay Audubon Sanctuary protects another 1,100 acres. Perhaps the most dramatic changes in the landscape have been from the continual erosion of the land from the battering of winter storms, and the growth of the forests. By the start of the 20th century, most of Wellfleet's forests were gone, due to shipbuilding, house construction, and fuel needs. Today much of the town is again wooded, as can be seen by the contemporary photographs taken for this book.

In 1930, the great Cape Cod historian Henry Kittredge wrote words that are as true of Wellfleet then as they are now: "Cape men and women take the goods the gods provide them. What, they argue, is the use of a proud history if it does not make them independent? . . . And the twinkle in their eyes, which [ship's captain] Grandfather Howes brought from the ends of the world and handed down to them with the teakwood blanket chest—that twinkle appears for a moment as they put the tourists' money in the till, and they chuckle at the ways of the world."

CHAPTER 1

VILLAGE STREETS

On any given morning, the only sounds in the village of Wellfleet are the ringing of the Congregational church bells and the answering chugs of fishing boats leaving the harbor below. Since 1850, when the church was built, this scene has remained virtually the same. Today an antique ship's clock rings from the steeple in eight-bell ship's time—recalling the great seafaring history of Wellfleet.

In the 1920s, cars driving the length of the Cape passed from the beginning of Main Street through the center of Wellfleet on the way to Provincetown. It was not until the 1950s that modern Route 6 bypassed Wellfleet Center, leaving the town and harbor with the look and character of an earlier era. (Vintage photograph courtesy of Michael Parlante.)

Entrance to Wellfleet
Cape Cod, Mass.

The approach to the center of Wellfleet is marked by a "Joseph's garden"—a dory stuffed with flowers and marked "Welcome to Wellfleet." Of such Cape Cod gardens, local lore says that the Reverend Joseph Metcalfe of Falmouth had two wishes in life: a new wig to replace the one "gnawed by silver-boterflies" and a boat of his own. But his congregation objected to such worldly desires. The new wig was barely tolerated, and the boat remained unused in Metcalfe's yard. One night a tempest uprooted the minister's rosebushes, landing them in his new dory—where they remained blooming until long after Metcalfe's death.

VILLAGE STREETS

High School & Congregational Church, Wellfleet, Mass.

In the 18th century, Wellfleet's small population was scattered in outlying villages, like Bound Brook Village to the north, Brook Village to the south, and the village on Billingsgate Island. By the 1880s, people had begun to migrate to the center village. Thus, as seen in this early-20th-century photograph, the Wellfleet high school was built in 1889, joining the union hall and Congregational church on Main Street.

In 1816, the first Methodist church in Wellfleet was built on Pleasant Hill, north of the village. After the great religious revivals in 1842–1843, a new church was built on Main Street. It was said to be the most elaborate church on the Cape at the time. Struck by lightning, it burned in 1891. A year later, Lorenzo Dow Baker financed the building that stands today. Noted English artist Claire Leighton designed the luminous stained glass in the church.

985. - M. E. Church, Main Street - WELLFLEET, Mass.

The substantial Sparrow house stood at the corner of Bank Street and Main Street until the 1920s. This two-family house had been shared by highly respected schoolteacher Mary Sparrow and the family of Austin C. Clark, the cashier of the Wellfleet Savings Bank.

By the 1920s, the Sparrow house was torn down, and in its place the center of Wellfleet was graced by a bandstand. To the right were a clapboard post office and Snow's ice-cream parlor and soda fountain. This area, at the corner of Bank Street and Main Street, is still the crossroads of Wellfleet Center.

By the 1940s, a First National grocery store was built on the site of the town bandstand. For a generation, Lema's Market made this building the center of Wellfleet's family food shopping. Next door was the town's only pharmacy, which left town in the 1990s. Today the Wellfleet Market has taken over the entire building and restored the striped awnings of the 1940s.

This 1930s photograph shows the Wellfleet Post Office on the left and Nye's Souvenir and Ice Cream Shop next door. Today the post office building houses the AIM Shop, which raises money for local health care. Some of the buildings in this row are among those moved into town from Great Island, Billingsgate Island, and Bound Brook Island in the 1880s. As early as 1850, Dr. William Stone saw the need for commercial buildings along Main Street and began moving buildings from declining Billingsgate.

MAIN STREET--BUSINESS SECTION WELLFLEET, MASS.

The Second Congregational Church was organized in South Wellfleet in 1833, beside what is now the South Wellfleet Cemetery. After the Civil War, the congregation, seeking a better location, moved temporarily into the Pond Hill schoolhouse. The church deteriorated and was bought in 1913 by the Daughters of the American Revolution. In about 1919, the building was moved to the center of Main Street where, in 1941, it became the Wellfleet Town Hall. After a fire in 1960 destroyed the building, the town replaced it with a replica.

The Isaiah Young house was barely saved from a terrible fire in 1908. It was the fire that cleared the way for today's town hall, wiping out a bakery, a barbershop, and a grocery store. Only wet blankets saved the Young house. Bank president Isaiah Young had built it, and later in the 1920s, Massachusetts governor Channing Cox used it as his summerhouse, where his guests included Pres. Calvin Coolidge. After serving many years as Aesop's Tables Restaurant, it has become the Winslow House Restaurant.

The famed Lighthouse Restaurant was known as Uncle Jim's in the 1940s. Moved from Great Island, the building has housed the post office (in the 1890s), the J. F. Rich ice-cream shop (1907), the Ship's Bell Restaurant (after 1936), and, for more than a generation, the Lighthouse Restaurant.

Our Lady of Lourdes Church was built on Main Street in 1912 and 1913. Catholics had celebrated mass in Wellfleet as early as 1877 in private homes. In 1900, an old schoolhouse on Route 6 was used until the church on Main Street could be built. In 1975, two itinerant artists, Charles McCleod and John Kendall, were allowed to tent in the churchyard of Our Lady of Lourdes. The men spent the summer there and hand-carved dramatic and colorful front doors. In the 1990s, the Catholic Church reorganized its facilities and sold the building to the Town of Wellfleet.

This view looks toward the center of town from the corner of Holbrook Avenue and Main Street. On the right is Henry S. Cook's Stoves, Hardware and Tin Shop. Today the building houses Eccentricities, a shop known for its remarkable clothing and goods from the Far East. Ironically, old Wellfleet would have been familiar with the store's stock from whaling days when ships set sail from here for the Pacific.

The Wellfleet Hotel stood on the southwest corner of Holbrook Avenue and Main Street. It was built in the 19th century as the Higgins family home. By 1905, railroad man James Pratt Smith was the owner. His wife, Hattie Viola, was a prolific poet, published in the *Cape Cod Item and Bee*. To the right was the Solomon Laha home. Solomon was the direct descendant of "Aunt Laha," a Wellfleet woman well known for having adopted 20 orphaned children during her nearly 96 years. In the early part of the 20th century, Clarence "Chicken" Ryder bought both buildings and turned them into the Wellfleet Hotel and the Annex. By the 1960s, the hotel was replaced by a post office.

David Rego has been a Wellfleeter since he was one week old. He provided this photograph taken on Howland Lane in June 1927. Two bicyclists, Ruth and Henry Littlefield, had just ridden about 100 miles to the Cape from Newton. Behind them are the barns of Rego's great-uncle Nelson Dyer, including an old schoolhouse on the left, in which Dyer stored hay. At the beginning of the Depression, a curtain factory was built there to employ local people who were out of work. That building is part of today's Wellfleet Public Library at the corner of Main Street.

The Depression-era curtain factory supplied Montgomery Ward and Sears. It was later transformed into the Colonial Candle factory. Two wings were added on Main Street for a candle retail shop on one side and a delicatessen on the other. In 1986, the town purchased the factory and converted it into a modern library. The Wellfleet Public Library was dedicated in early 1990. Here, in a photograph provided by library director Elaine McIlroy, women are seen lined up at sewing machines when the building was a curtain factory. The modern photograph shows library patrons lined up at computers in the same building,

When the railroad came to Wellfleet in 1870, it made the town accessible as a summer resort. Hotels like the Holbrook House (on Holbrook Avenue) and the Chequessett Inn (at Mayo's Beach) were built. Local transportation was handled by stables like Holbrook's Livery Stable, on the corner of Holbrook Avenue and Chequessett Neck Road. The Wellfleet annual report for 1901 lists 110 horses within town boundaries. Several blacksmiths, stablemen, and harness makers made their living in town at the time.

Chequesset Inn, Wellfleet, Mass.

This view from Holbrook Avenue shows the enormous Chequessett Inn, built on a pier over Wellfleet Harbor. On the hill to the right is the water tower for the inn. The Chequessett Inn was destroyed by a fierce late-winter storm in 1934. The *Boston Traveler* newspaper reported, "The four-story structure . . . buckled in the center as ice cakes pounded heavily at the base." Today the same view shows a mobile home park on land and Great Island on the other side of the harbor. (Vintage photograph courtesy of Michael Parlante.)

From Duck Creek, Bank Street rises toward Main Street. The building on the left, on the opposite side of Commercial Street, was Simeon Atwood's stove and hardware store. In the foreground on the left is the Wellfleet Marine Insurance Company (also called "the customs house"), and between the two small buildings, center, is the town pump. The Wellfleet Savings Bank, the large building with the mansard roof, was built in 1874, just after Wellfleet's greatest days as a fishing port. The Masonic temple of the Adams Lodge is in the trees on the right.

The town pump at the corner of Bank Street and Commercial Street was built in 1885. James Chandler provided the pump and labor for $23.50. David Holbrook's labor added another $1.60. Simeon Atwood's stove and hardware store provided the dipper and fixtures for $1.40, and the water trough was bought from O. H. Linnel for $41. This is the last remaining town pump. Other town pumps were at the intersection of Main Street and Holbrook Avenue, on Briar Lane, and in front of what was Alvin Paine's store in South Wellfleet.

1003. - The Town Pump and Masonic Hall - WELLFLEET, Mass.

In 1858, E. L. Collins built this apartment house on Commercial Street for seamen's families. He called it the Bradford Apartments, after his son Bradford. At the time, Collins was a successful carpenter, and he had his workshop and storage buildings across the street from the Bradford. Today this is the Bradford Condominiums.

The Bradford Apartments
Cape Cod
Wellfleet, Mass.

Catholic Church.   Wellfleet Mass.

Catholics from the Azores and Nova Scotia began settling in Wellfleet in the 1870s. In 1900, the town sold an old schoolhouse on Route 6 (opposite the cemeteries) to Henry Delory for $59. With that, the Catholics had their first chapel and established their first cemetery across the road. In 1912, they began building Our Lady of Lourdes on Main Street. Today a Mobil gas station occupies the site of the old schoolhouse/chapel on the corner of Route 6 and Main Street.

Birdseye View looking North from Congregational Church Tower, Wellfleet, Mass.

In the early part of the 20th century, a wonderful series of photographs was taken from the steeple of the Congregational church on Main Street. Thanks to the Congregational church and Denny O'Connell, contemporary photographs of the same views were also allowed to be taken from within the steeple. This early photograph takes in the view to the north, with Squire's Pond at left center. A similar photograph today attests to how much of Wellfleet's forests have grown back in the last 100 years.

This bird's-eye view from the steeple of the Congregational church shows the Methodist church to the west. The Methodist church steeple is the second one for the church, the first having burned to the ground after being struck by lightning in 1891.

This is a view of Uncle Tim's Bridge and treeless Hamblen Island. Beyond the island is the railroad dike, built across Duck Creek in 1870. Oyster shacks are seen by the dike. Uncle Tim's Bridge is still there, but the railroad dike is long gone.

Birdseye View Harbor and Railway Station from Congregational Church Tower, Wellfleet, Mass.

Looking southwest from the Congregational church steeple, a bit of Uncle Tim's Bridge and Hamblen Island can be seen on the far left. At left in the distance are the Lemon Pie Cottages and the town pier. Across the harbor is Indian Neck. In the center are buildings that are now Mac's Shack and the Bradford Condominiums, both on Commercial Street.

Wellfleet has a long tradition of Fourth of July parades. Here the town band advances down Main Street in the 1920s. In recent decades, the great wit and irony of modern Wellfleet has brought residents imaginative Fourth of July floats with themes like "the Mutant Ninja Quahogs" and novel parades, as seen here, of superhero kids.

CHAPTER 2

THE HARBOR

The best-known oyster shed in Wellfleet belonged to Marshall and Everett Higgins. It was on the east side of Commercial Street, by what is now the town marina. Here Lew Hatch, Commie Brown, and Sim Wiley shucked oysters, quahogs, and razorfish. The shed became known as the "Spit and Chatter Club." In 1959, it was moved across the street where its roof can still be seen in the center of what had been, until 2006, Captain Higgins' Restaurant. To the right were the Lemon Pie Cottages, yellow and the shape of pie slices. These had been brought to Wellfleet from the Yarmouth Campground by Capt. Lorenzo Dow Baker.

This view was taken some time after 1910 at the foot of Commercial Street, looking toward the town pier. The second oyster shed from the left is the Higgins "Spit and Chatter Club." On the far left is the Albert W. Davis Wholesale Scallop Company. Davis later became the manager of the Seal Shipped Oyster Company, whose buildings can be seen on the right. Davis's building became a blacksmith shop and was later moved to Drummer's Pond in South Wellfleet. The Seal Shipped Oyster Company sent huge quantities of famous Wellfleet oysters across the United States and Canada.

Atwood's Oyster House was at the end of Shirttail Point. In 1955, after 16 years of planning, a new town marina was built here. The tip of Shirttail Point was cut off during dredging, and now the marina's large parking lot covers the area. Until the new pier and marina were built, pleasure boats and the shellfishing fleet could access the harbor only at high tide. Today nearly 200 boats can be berthed here, and yachts from all over the eastern seaboard can be seen in the summertime.

The Higgins oyster shed (the "Spit and Chatter Club") is on the left. When the tide is low, remains of its piers can still be seen. Throughout the 19th century and into the 20th, mackerel, cod, oyster, scallop, and quahog sheds lined the shores of Duck Creek. On the right, the Lemon Pie Cottages can be seen on Milton Hill. A hurricane in the 1930s toppled and destroyed several of them.

THE HARBOR

The Wellfleet Harbor Actors Theater (WHAT) opened on the night of a blue moon, on July 31, 1985. Two nights later the town closed it down. Unfazed, the small company got the proper permits and went on with its first play, Eugène Ionesco's absurdist *Rhinoceros*. This was followed by more than 20 years of scalpel-sharp, daring plays in the little theater at the harbor. The company has premiered dozens of new works, several of which have gone on to Boston, New Haven, and New York. The *Boston Globe* recently said, "WHAT is not only the jewel in the Cape's crown, it is a jewel in Massachusetts's crown." The structure had been built by Al Graham around 1950. Over the years, it housed the Pub, the Harbor Inn, the Sundowner, and the legendary Uncle Frank's. Graham still occasionally haunts it. (Bartender Buster Bailey awoke one night to Graham's ghost in an upstairs room.) Today WHAT has a new state-of-the-art theater on Route 6, but it continues too in Al Graham's weathered beach shack at the harbor.

Uncle Tim's Bridge connects Hamblen Island to the village at East Commercial Street. The bridge was named for Timothy A. Daniels, who died in 1893 at the age of 86. On the left can be seen the steeple of the Methodist church. The house by the start of the bridge, now gone, was Daniels's ships' chandlery. The steeple of the Congregational church on Main Street is on the right.

Many schooners were built in this Duck Creek shipyard. Wellfleet was one of the Cape's largest whaling ports before the American Revolution. The first documented whaling schooner built in Wellfleet was the *Freemason*, built on Bound Brook Island in about 1800 and owned by Capt. Reuben Rich. This Duck Creek shipyard was begun by Henry Rogers and Sons. From 1848 to 1853, the company built eight schooners, the *Simeon Baker*, the *J. Y. Baker*, the *J. S. Higgs*, the *Benjamin Baker*, the *R. R. Freeman*, the *I. H. Horton*, the *George Shattuck*, and the *Varnum H. Hill*. Another shipbuilder, Nathaniel Snow, built two sloops for Capt. Lorenzo Dow Baker for the banana trade in Jamaica.

When the railroad came to Wellfleet in 1870, this railroad dike was built across Duck Creek, cutting off the town's inner harbor. With the railroad Wellfleet could easily ship its famous oysters to Boston, New York, and beyond. A cluster of oyster shacks can be seen along the dike. Today an abandoned wooden boat weathers on the remains of the dike.

The Mayo's Beach Lighthouse was built in 1880–1881 on Kendrick Avenue. Sarah Cleverly Atwood, the first woman to be appointed a keeper by the lighthouse service, was the first lighthouse keeper here. On March 10, 1922, the lighthouse was discontinued, and the next year the government sold it. The tower was torn down in 1939, but the house itself still stands. The small brick kerosene house remains behind the house, and, until recently, the cement circle of the lighthouse foundation could still be seen.

Capt. Lorenzo Dow Baker bought the old mercantile wharf on Mayo's Beach and in 1902 opened the elegant 62-room Chequessett Inn (on the far left, with the Mayo's Beach Lighthouse on the far right). The brochure stated that the "Chequessett Inn is built on the end of a spacious pier directly over the water . . . Our guests are sensible of the exhilarating conditions of a sea voyage with absolute exemption from its dangers. Beautiful Wellfleet Bay with its stretch of sand beach, creeks winding through green meadows, the picturesque village, Billingsgate Light and the Marconi towers, afford the sense and sight of never ending delights."

Chequessett Lily Pond View from Observatory looking West, Wellfleet, Mass.

This is a view from the bluff on Kendrick Avenue, just past the location of the Chequessett Inn. Later Kendrick was cut through to Chequessett Neck Road. Great Island can be seen on the left. In the center are the Mayo's Beach Bluff Cottages and next to them the distinctive tower house built by Capt. Lorenzo Dow Baker's son, Loren. Today trees shade the area from the hot sun.

Capt. Lorenzo Dow Baker made his fortune from fruit plantations in Jamaica and Central America. In Wellfleet he built the Chequessett Inn and in Jamaica the Titchfield Hotel at Port Antonio. He operated both hotels with the same Jamaican staff, since the Titchfield was open only in the winter and the Chequessett Inn only in the summer. Today only the stumps of the piers that supported the inn remain.

The Chequessett Inn became the location of the annual Regatta Day celebration. A typical Wellfleet yacht race was described in the *Barnstable Patriot* in May 1896: "The boats went over the course and careening around the buoys like seagulls on the wing . . . As all four boats in passing the buoy at starting were closely bunched together, the *Electra* broke her peak halyards, causing her to withdraw . . . The *Harolde* and the *Arawak* had a fine race, the former gaining by a slight margin." By 1921, swimming, yacht racing, and excellent dining were supplemented by billiards, tennis, and bowling at the inn.

Chequesset Inn. View from The Beach, Wellfleet, Mass.

The Bluff Cottages at Mayo's Beach were built by Capt. Lorenzo Dow Baker for overflow guests from his Chequessett Inn. The great American artist Edward Hopper took note of their exceptional architecture and immortalized the cottages in a 1933 watercolor titled *Cottages at Wellfleet*.

First Shovelfull on the new dyke, Aug. 7/08. Wellfleet, Mass.

On August 7, 1908, ground was broken for the Herring River dike on Chequessett Neck Road. The *Boston Herald* noted in 1907 that Wellfleet, "one of the prettiest towns on Cape Cod," was "stung" by mosquitoes and that vacationers were going elsewhere. With the building of the dike, the marsh was drained and the mosquitoes were controlled. Today the dike is a favorite spot for fishermen.

Pilot whales, known to Cape Codders as blackfish, used to enter Wellfleet Harbor in great numbers every fall. The Punanokanit Indians harpooned them in the water or drove them ashore. The Wellfleet Blackfish Company did the same thing. Their tryworks were located halfway between the town pier and the Mayo's Beach Lighthouse. Today when blackfish or dolphins get stranded in Wellfleet Harbor, great care is taken to return them to the sea. In 2005, the Cape Cod Stranding Network was called out to try to save a total of 315 dolphins and whales on Cape Cod. In this 1966 photograph a 65-foot finback whale that stranded on Mayo's Beach below the Bluff Cottages is seen. In the winter of 2005–2006, 72 dolphins and 18 pilot whales were swept to shore in Cape Cod Bay and were unable to return to the water independently.

THE HARBOR

Wellfleet's first children's summer camp was Camp Chequessett., a nautical camp for girls. It was founded in 1914 by Alice Belding and William Gould Vinal, off Nauhaught Bluff Road. The brochure stated, "The location on Cape Cod lends a charm and zest that only the tang of salt air, and sparkle of sunshine on sandy beach and blue water can add to a summer's fun. Salt water means a world of adventure. Swimming and diving in the warm protected water at camp, surf bathing, games and picnics on magnificent sandy beaches, and even cruising and deep-sea fishing may be shared by all . . . The equipment includes practically every kind of craft, from camper-made-rafts to canoes, rowboats, sailing dories, and the 40' cabin cruiser 'Mouette.' Activities at camp are alternated with trips to inland fresh water ponds, surf bathing on the 'Back Shore,' and cruises on 'Mouette' to Plymouth, Provincetown, and occasionally to farther ports on Buzzards Bay and Nantucket Sound . . . $325 a season." Today the Camp Chequessett main house can still be seen on Nauhaught Bluff. (Vintage photograph courtesy of Michael Parlante.)

Camp Chequessett provided idyllic summers for girls for 14 years, beginning in 1914. "Cap'n Bill," William Gould Vinal, became the president of the National Association of Directors of Girls' Camps in 1920. He and Alice Belding (of Vassar) trained thousands of girls in natural history, and many went on to careers as nature recreation leaders. One camper, Elizabeth Bishop, known as "Bishie," became one of this country's finest poets. Bishop's early poems were printed in the *Camp Chequessett Log*, the camp's newsletter. She later won both a Pulitzer Prize and a National Book Critics Circle Award. The 1923 photograph shows campers about to go sailing. Today the beach they set sail from is overlooked by summer homes. (Vintage photograph courtesy of Michael Parlante.)

THE ISLANDS

Great Island was originally inhabited by the Punanokanits, and the remains of their clam and oyster mounds can still be seen. In 1970 and 1971, archaeologists from Plimoth Plantation studied the site of Samuel Smith's tavern on the island. The tavern's heyday was from 1690 through 1740. They discovered fragments of wine bottles, broken wineglasses, whale bones, a harpoon shaft, scrimshaw, a lady's ivory fan, and part of a man's skull that had been cleaved by an ax. The early-20th-century hunters in this photograph enjoyed the island as well.

GUNNING CAMP, GREAT ISLAND, WELLFLEET, MASS.

The Gunner's Camp on Great Island was popular in the years before the island became part of the National Seashore. These "coot" hunters display their catch on the wall of the cabin. Coot, today called scoters, migrate to the area in the fall. The men lured them in using pig bladders as decoys. Coot stew was a popular dish. Today Great Island is peaceful and uninhabited. Shellfish fishermen cultivate beds of oysters on the flats with Great Island as a background.

Wellfleet's most mysterious island was Billingsgate. By 1935, it completely disappeared beneath the sea. For generations the island had been the site of nearly 30 homes, wharves, a school, and a lighthouse. Early on, Native Americans had lived there, and in December 1620, the Pilgrims noted Billingsgate Island as they explored Cape Cod Bay. At low tide, the foundations of the lighthouse can still be found on the lost island.

These photographs show a rustic homestead on Billingsgate Island and a scattering of chimney bricks that are left today. In 1822, the first lighthouse was built on Billingsgate Island. It was only the third one on Cape Cod, preceded by one in Truro and one in Provincetown. The sea battered the island, and the lighthouse had to be repaired in 1854, and then replaced completely in 1858. During a storm in 1875, lighthouse keeper Herman Dill wrote, "I do not know but the Island will All wash away." On March 26, 1876, Dill wrote, "The very worst storm for the winter was Last Night." He was found dead in the lighthouse dory the following day. By 1910, the lighthouse was uninhabitable.

THE ISLANDS

As the island eroded, several of the Billingsgate houses and oyster sheds were taken off on barges to become landmarks in other parts of Wellfleet. Down from about 50 acres to barely 5, the island was deserted, except for Emil Poikonen, the island's last inhabitant. After Poikonen returned to his native Finland, the island was left to the birds and seals. Today it is a shoal, but when it becomes visible at low tide, ghostly remains of the old days return, like these stumps of one of the island's many piers.

VIEW AT BROWN BROOK ISLAND WELLFLEET MASS. 113

While Billingsgate Island was disappearing, other Wellfleet islands became part of the mainland as the marshes that surrounded them silted in. Bound Brook Island was one, along with Great Island and Griffin Island. There had been at least 16 homes and a schoolhouse on Bound Brook Island. It was home to such notables as Capt. Lorenzo Dow Baker and to Nehemiah Somes Hopkins, who became a medical missionary to China. Today, fully connected to the mainland, Bound Brook has become a mysterious wooded hill.

CHAPTER 4

THE GREAT BEACH
AND THE PONDS

BEACH VIEW NEAR COAST GUARD STATION,
WELLFLEET, CAPE COD, MASS.

489

In the 1850s, Henry Thoreau wrote of the outer beaches of Wellfleet, "Today it was the Purple Sea, an epithet which I should not before have accepted. There were distinct patches of the color of a purple grape with the bloom rubbed off. But first and last the sea is of all colors . . . Commonly, in calm weather, for half a mile from the shore, . . . the sea is green . . . as are some ponds; then blue for many miles, often with purple tinges, bounded in the distance by a light, almost silvery stripe; beyond which there is generally a dark blue rim . . . Thus we sat on the foaming shore, looking on the wine-colored ocean." In contrast, Wellfleet's ponds are remarkably clear, deep, and blue. They are of the rare type called kettle ponds, created during the ice age when glaciers left huge chunks of ice on the Cape as they retreated.

In 1872, the U.S. Life Saving Service was created. Along Cape Cod, nine Coast Guard stations were built where a keeper was stationed year-round and where large crews lived from August through May each year. The Cahoon's Hollow station had two surfboats to send out to save men in shipwrecks. This surfboat is being pulled back up on the beach by a horse. Today's U.S. Coast Guard saves lives with 47-foot rescue boats, Jay Hawk helicopters, Falcon jets, and C-130 aircraft.

Surf Boat Drill.

Photograph Copyrighted 1906 by H.J. Robbins, Boston.

THE GREAT BEACH AND THE PONDS

The Cahoon's Hollow Life Saving Station still stands on the dunes. Pictured here are members of an early crew and their wives. From left to right are Ed Lombard (kneeling) and his wife, a Mr. Ennis, Mrs. Cook and Al Cook, and Asa Lombard (kneeling). The Coast Guard built the station in 1893, after a fire destroyed the original building. Today it is the Beachcomber restaurant and club, known for its great music, dance floor, flowing beer, outdoor bar, and the crashing Atlantic Ocean at the bottom of the dune. For over 20 years, Chandler Travis and the Incredible Casuals have played here every Sunday night in the summer months. From left to right are Steve Wood, Chandler Travis, Johnny Spampinato, Rikki Bates, Aaron Spade, and Lou McMurrer. (Vintage photograph courtesy of the National Seashore Archives.)

Between the 1890s and the 1930s, Wellfleet made a transition from being solely a seafaring village to one that included summer homes and an arts community. Families like that of Eugene Noble Foss could afford to stay at inns and boardinghouses here or to build their own pondside camps, as the Foss family did on Duck Pond. Foss, born in Vermont in 1858, made his fortune in the manufacture of iron and steel products after moving to Boston in 1882. He served in the U.S. Congress in 1910 and was governor of Massachusetts from 1911 to 1913. This chart from 1901 shows Wellfleet's many glacial ponds, with Duck Pond just below Great Pond. The modern photograph is of Duck Pond today.

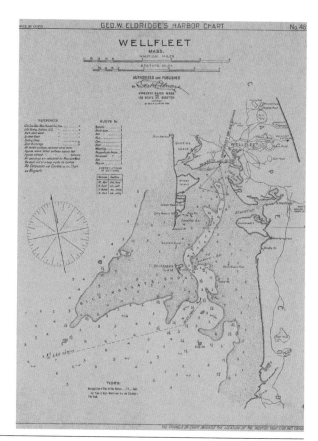

On June 17, 1857, Henry Thoreau observed in his journal, "There were two or three . . . of those peculiar ponds, with high, shiny sand-banks, by which you detected them before you saw the water, as if freshly scooped out of the high plains . . .. The banks were like those of the sea on the Back Side, though on a smaller scale, and they had clear sandy shores. One pond would often be separated from another by low curving beaches or necks of land." This early postcard shows Great Pond separated from North East Pond by a neck of land, just as Thoreau described. All of the ponds surrounding Great Pond today (North East, South East, and Turtle Ponds), were once merely bays of Great Pond until shore drifting built silt bars across them.

NORTH EAST AND GREAT PONDS, WELLFLEET, MASS.

During the ice age, each new glacier pushed rocks and sand over blocks of ice that had been left by previous glaciers. When melted, the ice blocks left enormous depressions that were later filled by groundwater. Some of these clear, pure ponds were used in the 19th century to harvest ice. These photographs of Long Pond show summertime swimmers in 1937 near the ramp used to harvest ice in the winter and the public beach at the pond today. (Vintage photograph courtesy of Michael Parlante.)

Ice harvesters are seen cutting blocks of ice on a Wellfleet pond (probably Long Pond) to store for the summer. Blocks were kept in icehouses, each block insulated from the next with a thick layer of hay and sawdust. Fishermen needed ice to use in the shipping of their catch, but even more than ice they needed massive quantities of salt to cure fish to ship even greater distances. In 1837, Wellfleet had 39 saltworks that produced a total of 18,000 bushels of salt. Each saltworks used small windmills to draw seawater into large pans. Sea salt was left after a period of solar evaporation.

"Alone" Gull Pond, Wellfleet, Mass.

After naturalist Henry Thoreau stayed with a Wellfleet oysterman in the mid-1800s, he recalled, "Our host took pleasure in telling us the names of the ponds, most of which we could see from his windows, and making us repeat them after him, to see if we had got them right. They were Gull Pond, the largest and a very handsome one, clear and deep, and more than a mile in circumference, Newcomb's, Swett's, Slough, Horse-Leech, Round, and Herring Ponds . . . Innumerable gulls used to resort to them; but the large gulls were now very scarce, for, as he said, the English robbed their nests far in the north, where they breed." Here a postcard of Gull Pond is paired with a broad view of the pond today.

CHAPTER 5

SOUTH WELLFLEET

BUSINESS CENTRE, SOUTH WELLFLEET, MASS.

The center of South Wellfleet was built at Blackfish Creek where space for good wharves was available. Beyond the wharves residents fished the tidal flats of the bay, which were rich in clams, oysters, and scallops. In 1833, 42 members of the first church withdrew to form the Second Congregational Church in South Wellfleet. The hamlet prospered, and eventually there were several schools, two churches, a post office, and a railroad station. Its little center sits back from Route 6 at the corner of Lecount Hollow Road. The highway and the railroad used to pass right through the village center. Now Route 6 bypasses it, and the railroad is a bike path. Yet a market, shops, and the post office still remain.

In the center distance of this postcard of South Wellfleet center are the towers of the Marconi Wireless Station, built in 1902. On the left is Isaac Paine's general store, and in the distant right is the railroad station. Gasoline could be bought at the building on the right for the first cars that came through, beginning in 1905. In "My Cape Cod Memories," Ethel M. Paine recalls, "Those days everything revolved around high tide, when everyone went to the beach for a swim or a wade . . . everyone went to the depot at train-time—walked of course—then waited while the stationagent-mailclerk sorted the mail. Moonlight nights all would trek over to the Back Shore by the Marconi Wireless Station for a picnic supper on the beach, around a huge bonfire made of driftwood. Then all would join in the song-fest, during which time the Coast Guard Patrol would come by and stop with us a few minutes before resuming patrol. Often, too, part of the Marconi staff would come down to join us."

A little dog—a mascot of the Marconi Wireless Station crew—poses in the trough of the South Wellfleet town pump. In the background is the small railroad depot, built when the railroad first came to Wellfleet in 1870. In the 1930s, William Sexton dismantled the depot and moved it to land he owned on Blackfish Creek. When Robert and Susan Gross bought the place in February 1976, it was a mere shell. They spent 10 weekends working on it. On July 10, the Grosses moved in for the summer. Camping on the floor, they put up sheetrock and made it into a home. Susan (seen here by the modernized and expanded building) and her husband retired to their place on Barker Road in 1996.

ROAD LEADING TO CANNON HILL CAMP, S. WELLFLEET, MASS.

Wellfleet Center and South Wellfleet both have places known as "Cannon Hill." The South Wellfleet one, shown here, is at Cannon Hill Road, off Route 6. The other Cannon Hill is also known as Hamblen Island and is reached by way of Uncle Tim's Bridge on Commercial Street. At one time, both hills had cannons, but where they came from is a mystery. Local historian Earle Rich believed they might have come from the British Revolutionary War frigate called *Somerset*. Myra Hicks thought the cannons came from a British ship during the War of 1812. Hicks lived at the South Wellfleet Cannon Hill. Her father had been one of the boys who stole the Hamblen Island cannon as a prank in 1908. It was said there was a 100-year-long tradition of Wellfleet and South Wellfleet stealing and hiding the last remaining cannon (the other having been lost). For 30 years, Myra Hicks kept the secret of its location—buried in her yard. Today the cannon is on the lawn in front of the Wellfleet Town Hall on Main Street.

Turn down Paine Hollow Road off Route 6 and the road will lead to the aptly named Point Pleasant. Wharves used to stretch from the point until about 1878, when the larger ships that became common bypassed the shallow waters there. Located within Blackfish Creek, the rich tidal flats attracted shellfish fishermen and the view attracted summer cottages. Today trees and wooden barriers help slow the erosion of Point Pleasant.

In 1889, at the age of 16, Guglielmo Marconi sent a wireless electrical signal across his mother's garden in Bologna, Italy. On the night of January 18, 1903, Marconi made world history in South Wellfleet when he transmitted the first transatlantic wireless message to England—a message from Pres. Theodore Roosevelt to King Edward VII in London. Today the Marconi Wireless Station site is within the Cape Cod National Seashore.

Arthur Tuckerman, part of the Marconi crew, walks the Marconi mascots with the transmission towers in the distance. The four towers were 210 feet high and set in a 200-foot square. Each tower was 24 feet square at the base and 8 feet square at the top. Twelve steel cables, one inch thick, secured each tower against high winds. The guy wires were anchored to 12-inch-by-12-inch crossed timbers buried 9 feet deep in the sand. The cables were tightened by giant turnbuckles and insulated with ships' deadeyes, rubber hoses, and manila rope. A model of the tower complex is in a Plexiglas case at the site.

Many of the Marconi crew members were local Cape Codders, the riggers who built the towers, cooks, carpenters, and so on. When King Edward VII responded to Pres. Theodore Roosevelt's transatlantic message, his reply was given to Wellfleet man Charlie Paine to take to the South Wellfleet railroad depot. From there it was transferred by telegraph to Washington, D.C. Paine's wagon and his horse, Diamond, had been in Marconi's service from the beginning of construction. He became a local celebrity and often told the story of the day Guglielmo Marconi gave him the famous message and told him to "drive like the wind," promising Paine, "If your horse falls dead, I'll buy you another." Paine later revealed, "'Twas four mile hard goin' and I wasn't going to kill my horse for nobody."

This early postcard shows the remains of one of the four-foot-thick cement slabs used as a base for the transmission towers. Marconi had bought eight acres of highlands in South Wellfleet from Ed Cook for $250 and set himself up to live in the Holbrook House, on Holbrook Avenue. His first antenna, built of 20 ships' masts in 1901, was blown down in a storm on November 25, 1901. By December 11, 1902, four massive wooden towers replaced them.

BEACH VIEW, CAPE COD, MASS.   483

Below, Guglielmo Marconi poses at the wireless station. From here, Pres. Theodore Roosevelt's message was sent to identical towers on the shore at Poldhu, England. His message read, "In taking advantage of the wonderful triumph of scientific research and ingenuity which has been achieved in perfecting a system of wireless telegraphy, I extend on behalf of the American People most cordial greetings and good wishes to you and to all the people of the British Empire." In 1999, Princess Elettra Marconi came from Rome to Wellfleet for the 125th anniversary of her father's birth.

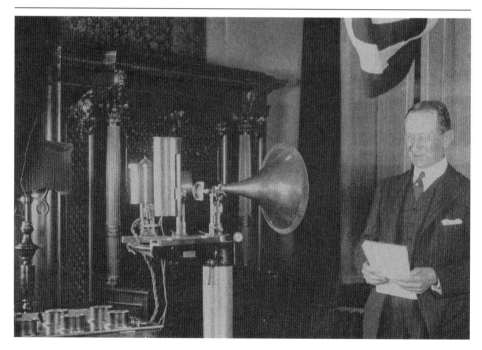

On March 19, 1943, Camp Wellfleet was opened in South Wellfleet, on four miles of what is now Marconi Beach. It was the antiaircraft artillery training center for Camp Edwards (later named Otis Air Force Base) on the Upper Cape. Men were sent from Camp Edwards to train on the firing range of Camp Wellfleet, the former site of the Marconi Wireless Station. This photograph shows the antiaircraft artillery on the beach firing at target planes over the water. Empty shell casing can occasionally be found on the beach, despite several cleanup efforts. (Vintage photograph courtesy of Michael Parlante.)

"Fat Jack" and "Henry" pose in front of the military police building at Camp Wellfleet. Built at a cost of $400,000, the camp had 17 single-story barracks that housed 50 men each. There were four company administration and supply buildings, five lavatory buildings, an assembly hall that held 400, an infirmary, a post exchange, an ammunition magazine, a storehouse, and a firefighting unit. Today little but this helicopter landing pad remains. (Vintage photograph courtesy of Michael Parlante.)

The field kitchen at Camp Wellfleet fed the men when they were training to fire artillery on the beach. The camp also had five complete mess halls capable of seating 200 men. Local newspapers recorded the domestic side of the soldiers' lives. A newspaper from March 23, 1944, states, "Master Sergeant Francis Maggiacomo and the Mrs. have had an infant they aptly labeled 'Francis Jr,' while T/5 Raymond Westergaard of the Record Section recently married a Cape Cod lovely who resided at Eastham." (Vintage photograph courtesy of Michael Parlante.)

Men training as antiaircraft gunners at Camp Wellfleet prepared a target plane to fly over the Atlantic off Marconi Beach. Wellfleet aquaculturist and collector Michael Parlante located this wooden propeller from one of the Camp Wellfleet target planes. In 1961, the site was declared excess and conveyed to the Department of the Interior by Pres. John F. Kennedy as part of the Cape Cod National Seashore.

CHAPTER 6

INNS, HOTELS,
AND THE RAILROAD

43001 Yacht Race Day at Chequesset Inn, Wellfleet, Mass.

Wellfleet's golden age of summer hotels and inns was ushered in by the coming of the railroad in 1870 and firmly established when automobile travel became feasible in the second decade of the 20th century. With many Americans turning from fishing and farming to industry, the middle and wealthy classes grew, and places like Wellfleet became desirable resorts. Grand hotels like the Chequessett Inn (above) and the Indian Neck Hotel flourished. They rented rooms on "the American plan," which included room and board, and guests stayed for weeks, often months, at a time.

A winter ice storm froze Wellfleet Harbor in February 1934. The wharf under the Chequessett Inn, strong enough to hold 62 rooms and the automobiles of guests, was undermined by the ice floes. The inn crumbled, and all that remains today are the pilings on which it once stood. These can still be seen at low tide at Mayo's Beach, offshore from the point where Kendrick Avenue turns sharply away from the beach. Note the shard of Chequessett Inn china (below).

INNS, HOTELS, AND THE RAILROADS

On November 30, 1870, the *Provincetown Advocate* announced the coming of the Wellfleet railroad: "We understand that the citizens of Wellfleet are making arrangements for a grand Railroad opening . . . They are to be aided and assisted by Superintendent Winslow who will extend an invitation to the Stockholders of the Cape Cod Railroad to be present, and a rich treat is anticipated. The people of this live, go-ahead town know how to do up these things in good style." The depot stood at Commercial Street, opposite the foot of Railroad Avenue, near today's Sandpiper Gallery.

This scene is on Railroad Avenue, looking toward Commercial Street and the railroad depot. Soon after the railroad opened in Wellfleet, the local newspaper wrote that "the varieties of the 'toot' of the locomotive, and gyrations of the arms of the conductors by day, or lanterns by night are about as intelligent to most people as first class Choctaw . . . One whistle—down brakes. Two whistles—off brakes. Three whistles—back up. Continuous whistles—danger. A rapid succession of short whistles is the cattle alarm, at which the brakes will always be put down. A sweeping parting of hands on level of eyes, is a signal to go ahead. A downward motion of the hand, with extended arms, to stop. A beckoning motion of one hand, to back. A lantern raised and lowered vertically, is a signal for starting, swung at right angles or crossways the track, 'stop,' swung in a circle, 'back the train.' A red flag waved upon the track must be regarded as a signal of danger. Hoisted at the station, it is a signal for a train to stop. Carried unfurled upon an engine, it is a warning that another engine or train is on its way."

INNS, HOTELS, AND THE RAILROADS

In 1871, the Holbrook House on Holbrook Avenue was described in the *Barnstable Patriot* as "the most home-like Hotel in the State . . . as a natural sequence it is always well filled with a crowd of delighted guests. Mr. and Mrs. [Henry] Holbrook are pre-eminently qualified for the hotel business, have had large experience, and know just how to make all who patronize them feel at home—and that is the great secret of hotel keeping." No longer standing, it was across from the beginning of Chequessett Neck Road. In 1901, Guglielmo Marconi set up his first local headquarters here. In 1903, reporters from around the world stayed at the Holbrook House while Marconi sent the first wireless communication to Europe from his station in South Wellfleet. Opposite the Holbrook House can be seen the Holbrook's Livery Stable.

In 1812, Capt. Jesse Holbrook built this house at the beginning of Main Street. In the 1930s, Joseph and Lalie Price of Philadelphia converted it into the grand Holiday House hotel. In the renovation, the Prices used lumber from the Chequessett Inn, which had crumbled into the harbor, and columns from the ruins of the Libby mansion. The grand columns were put on the back of the house, in mistaken anticipation that the new Route 6 would pass close to that side. It did not, but the columns can still be seen at the back of the inn. Today this is the popular Inn at Duck Creeke.

Every day, in the early years of the 20th century, a freight train filled with fish waited on a sidetrack of the Wellfleet depot for the northbound train to pass. After the train came through, the freight train would continue its journey from Provincetown to Boston. In the early summer of 1908, as the northbound train chugged toward the depot, a switch was accidentally turned and the locomotive barreled onto the sidetrack and crashed into three freight cars filled with mackerel. It was said that the steam escaping from the engine cooked the mackerel. The present-day photograph shows the abandoned railroad dike that approached the depot.

Here a boy inspects the 1908 train wreck. The day after the wreck, a crew arrived from Middleboro to restore rail service to Wellfleet and Provincetown. During the salvage operation, an exploding gasoline lantern ignited the clothing of one of the workmen helping raise the locomotive to an upright position. The son of the Middleboro crew foreman, he, sadly, died. A photograph taken from the steeple of the Congregational church on Main Street shows (in the foreground) where the railroad depot stood.

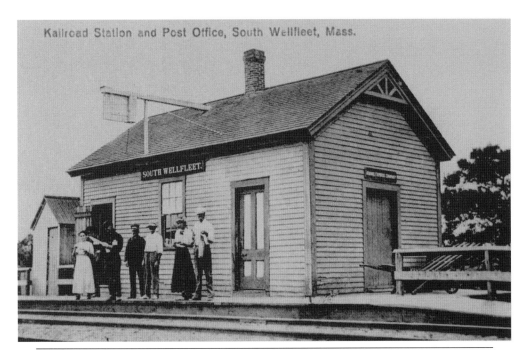

Railroad Station and Post Office, South Wellfleet, Mass.

Ethel M. Paine recalled arriving at the South Wellfleet train station, near the corner of Route 6 and Lecount Hollow Road, in the early part of the 20th century. As a child, she and her family left Worcester for Boston by train and then took a boat from Boston across Cape Cod Bay to Provincetown. The train ride from Provincetown to South Wellfleet was a "very dusty, slow ride." Of her arrival, she wrote, "I remember the lovely sweet breaths of sea-washed air perfumed with the scent of pine that we inhaled deeply when we stepped off the train." The depot stood beside what is today the bicycle rail trail behind the South Wellfleet General Store.

After many hours of travel, visitors arrived at the South Wellfleet depot for an unforgettable summer. Ethel M. Paine wrote, "Those days folks came down when school closed and stayed all summer, and everyone got to know every one else . . . Sailing was the most coveted pleasure, and the very few families on Lieutenant's Island had to sail either to Wellfleet or our Stubbs' landing on Blackfish Creek for mail and supplies . . . A horse and buggy could be hired at Wellfleet for a boy to take his girl for a ride. When a group of us packed a picnic lunch and went in a buckboard to Highland Light and Provincetown, that was the outing event of the season . . . Or to go sailing down to Billinsgate Island Light and stay over the tide for a swim and dig for clams and picnic was something to write home about." Today a tourist information booth sits across from where the depot stood.

INNS, HOTELS, AND THE RAILROADS

The elegant summer days of the Chequessett Inn are gone. Yet today a sunset at Mayo's Beach, with the sound of "eight bells" ringing from the church steeple and the sight of fishing boats returning to the harbor, can blur the difference between then and now.

ACROSS AMERICA, PEOPLE ARE DISCOVERING SOMETHING WONDERFUL. *THEIR HERITAGE.*

Arcadia Publishing is the leading local history publisher in the United States. With more than 3,000 titles in print and hundreds of new titles released every year, Arcadia has extensive specialized experience chronicling the history of communities and celebrating America's hidden stories, bringing to life the people, places, and events from the past. To discover the history of other communities across the nation, please visit:

www.arcadiapublishing.com

Customized search tools allow you to find regional history books about the town where you grew up, the cities where your friends and family live, the town where your parents met, or even that retirement spot you've been dreaming about.